torch song tango choir

Camino del Sol

A Latina and Latino Literary Series

torch song tango choir

Julie Sophia Paegle

THE UNIVERSITY OF ARIZONA PRESS

TUCSON

www.uapress.arizona.edu

Library of Congress Cataloging-in-Publication Data
appear on the last printed page of this book.

Publication of this book is made possible in part by the proceeds of a permanent endowment created with
the assistance of a Challenge Grant from the National Endowment for the Humanities, a federal agency.

Manufactured in the United States of America on acid-free, archival-quality paper containing a minimum of
30% post-consumer waste and processed chlorine free.

15   14   13   12   11   10   6   5   4   3   2   1

for my parents, Julia Nogues Paegle and Jan Paegle,

and their parents, Alejandro Nogues and Julia Elvira Acuña de Nogues,

Alfred Dinne and Antonia Dinne,

and Elmars Paegle,

wherever you may be

Contents

tango liso

choir

The bandoneón is an accordion-like musical instrument originally created in Europe to provide missionaries with portable organ music for religious services in remote locales, particularly in the Americas. But when the instrument immigrated to Argentina around 1885, it was adopted by tango musicians to create the tango's characteristic sound.

torch song tango choir

Canto de Abril

for Julia Elvira Acuña de Nogues, April 11, 1919–March 25, 2008

Pianoforte played from the old house drifted to the plaza where we'd hear
Which songs did you play, Abuela?　　*Torch songs tangos zambas　　the occasional nocturne*
when toads are troubadours　　crickets chorus half-light　　far from Buenos Aires　　near

that city's vicious litanies　churning from Plaza de Mayo　　*they trailed us year after year*
turned folksong by our caserón antiguo　　*we all hid here*　　where jasmine greets fern
and yuccas stalk ocelots　　What did you hide from?　　*From how else to disappear*

from how others' silences would bloom　　could deafen　　then sudden how their voices would flare
Tío's bandoneón's warnings or cats' keening　　*nightly those low notes' lantern*
crossed rivers from a far square　　Where did you hide?　　*Far from the Plaza near*

revolution always near war　　which seek like a song a half-lunatic turn in half-light carried on the air
buried deep in song between a square a street a prayer a dance any verse might turn
years to good　　life too dim without illusion　　our camp's sad magics

for a while to disappear

Inside the Bandoneón

for Pedro Sofiel Acuña, March 30, 1917–June 23, 2003

Sometimes tenements transpire between
bass and descant, left and right hand.

In some reeds, concertina occasion-
ally meets accordion while

in bellow, a box haunts crosswind.
Usually each unbuttoned

pull greets its push come clean,
and all this starts small to always recall

when mission music spilled,
five octaves went new-world wild.

And now? Palm the moving hungers
that psalm dance halls sublime,

and pull: twilight's when the fingers
follow in their other time.

torch songs

Y todo a Media Luz, que es un brujo el amor

—*Carlos César Lenzi and Edgardo Donatto, "A Media Luz"*

Good-bye Love Song with Siroopwafelen

It was everything amber: all butter and hot
honeyed rum running out and dripping from
that fall's taut, punched-out honeycomb.
It was canal and street and dam within the knot

and crumble of Amsterdam. It was bergamot.
Burned toast. Steeped tea. A boat in a poem
(or its possibility). Quarrel and chrysanthemum.
It was always wet (so were we). And so? What

of what it would not be: always autumn. Now,
a mile above sea level, eyes closed, I see the maze
of dikes, the knack they have for sure upend-

ing of lands from under the sea. The why the how
the who (the her) I send them all, walled if near, from praise
of what we were (you, me) before the end unopened.

Torch Song for Ophelia

       Forget
about Hamlet.
       He required too much: air,
Purgatory, his harpy/whore,
       revenge,

       stories
on stories—one
       play not enough
for him; take heart—the dog will have
       his day.

       Lady,
let us make love.
       The thrust and tumult have
only just begun. See what we
       see: your

       fair form,
reflected in
       our thousand waters—woe
blasted with ecstasy. Come in,
       come in,

        adown
among the waves;
             you, a creature native
to this element. Down, let us
             drink you;

             water
won't care, only
             riddle itself more fierce-
ly where more mermen have barely been;
             enter,

             dive in
on wish-ridden
             sea horses envying star-
fish the patient radial
             love of

             their beds—
But we'll envy
             their envy no longer,
no less—Now leave the weeping
             willow,

             O maid
Ophelia,
             spread your dress—and you, O

you, you mad, damned darling,
        yield your-

        self all
ways and always
        are met, on this under-
side of madness, and are riant,
        and wet.

Chessboard Ghazal

for Alejandro Nogues, April 28, 1906–October 5, 1989

On our map of Aconcagua, red lines sunder a better name.
Rain on topo. Penned landslides plunder the better name.

Lightning runs the metropolitan air, then lingers on its aim.
Ciudad de Cúpulas, Buenos Aires. But thunder's a better name.

Before Perón, they courted among roses, yuccas still aflame.
In the plaza's corner, he proposed. She declined her better name.

Argentina's grand master (my grandfather) died in an endgame.
What world hovered beyond his board, I wonder? *A better name.*

Homelands lost, a generation fading: whom will the children claim?
Are the unborn in time to gather us together under a better name?

Good-bye Love Song with Oil Painting by Randall Lake

Since I gave away your portrait, "Rococo
Punk," I've been seeing your ghost, fleshed-out, Baroque—
unpuckering an unlucky Marlboro;
attempting ten red temples in your spiked mohawk—
these, and a Coke can, slightly soften the shock
of copper brocade clambering up the obese armchair
that held your slim-hipped sittings, Fridays, five o'clock,
of that sudden spring in high school and your first love affair:
with socialism, Aqua Net, all things threadbare,
and Robyn Wall. And Robyn Wall ten years ago taught me to adore
elaborately all that you loved, the better to bear
my narrow desire as broad witness before
the crazy wealth of this world, in which I wish you'd stay
a small time more, until I grow accustomed to giving you away.

Paean
The prejudiced goat

is nonetheless unfuss-
y about precipice—

lip vs. ledge, crag vs. the if
of mica-flaked cliff—

so long as a hoof-span of granite
is less than a blissed-out bleat-

ing leap away. Then there is
the rebutting of hunches

(this path, that path) made
between twin eclipses gasped

jagged, shadow crescents splayed
knee-keep, in gray-bladed

tangle across tall grass.
There is something crass

in all overlap. Hello
volcano. Hello nightshade.

Paean

The implacable alpaca

will not be scolded. Nor aid a scolding. Not for some atmospheric wrath,
spluttering his twister, all piss and vinegar. She *knows* Behemoth,

and he can do better than this (sidekick to a sandbag and a monstrous
pet). She's had it with floods and droughts, this maker's hit-and-miss bias

—all bets are off. On the horizon, shimmering low, there's a promise,
a hover, some better myth in which she has her own rosy apotheosis,

along with generously cut sequined robe, yards of satin, fashioning largess
into a straight, red road—which she follows, stampeding straight out of Job.

Tanda con Cortes
Little Break from Recoleta Cemetery

Beaten by heat and by florid death, we stumble
through Iglesia de Nuestra Señora de Pilar,
half-blind, avoiding the looming outlines
of curtains, statues, worship's furniture

as we lurch to the pew where we avoid
the question: why return to Recoleta each year?
Inner city to Buenos Aires' best-connected dead—
No one we know is buried here.

And it's always an almost tropical enero near noon,
with altars losing bricks while epitaphs go black
and roses open rhodochrosite, while we regret
the family we still haven't seen—briefly close and living—

trying to silence our footfalls, to hush
the abrupt thud of the knee rest
as we cool in the pews, but then a voice: *¿De los estados?*
Been through the cemetery yet?

The stranger's sudden, named Jorge, up today
from Tierra del Fuego—Ushuaia, far south—
and you clear your throat to indicate—what?—
the quiet, polite code from which his mouth

strays, though it closes around *Jorge*, lips chiseled
after *Fuego*. How can it be, in the gloom and the hush,
that his voice whispers insistent but not from him,
that now his stories emerge as all voices vanish,

that finally what remains is an unsettled, insistent din—
where did his stories go? Could it be that the statues
eat his words, holding them like wafers
on thick plaster tongues, which share their edges

with throats, with teeth and palates and vocal cords beyond—
all filled to the blur of a statue's anatomy, which must
petrify all it takes in. Outside, voices rise:
wind, tamboril, human—although the song's words are lost

to the street's roar—the edges of verse already blurred
by their abundance and by their pass through wall
and window and stained glass, back into air where Jorge
whispers the lot with a voice on loan—he tells it all—

each murmur another's secret, a disappearance shown,
—*all cities are cemeteries*—this stranger's complaint,
there—can you taste it?—between lips, your own,
swallowed by the sad, solid mouths of demon and saint,

the virgins, the passions, pietàs, and wraiths—
they lack echo and hollow, they cannot dissolve,
except in their cracks, which whisper their famine—
and even from those they take in, they take in.

Little Break from Iglesia de Nuestra Señora de Pilar

Thank God for the beaver pond.
          I had my own doubts about cutting our two-hour
                    trail so close to the pond, but those animals

are not shy, and let me tell you: it was destiny.
          Last night, I guided two men. They said they'd
                    come to Tierra del Fuego because they

had a task to fulfill. They needed a place,
          far south, where animals live with water.
                    We arrived at the pond. I tied the horses.

The men went ahead, beyond the trees.
          Just as I finished uncinching,
                    I knew what their task was.

The last cinch dangled, dark and warm,
          close to its shadow on the loam, and it hit me:
                    They are scattering ashes. I knew.

I stayed away. I watched the cinch sway.
          Since then, this has walked beside me,
                    even through the cemetery today:

A man's body, his whole life,
      has come to this end, here, in this pond,
            with these men and the horses and me.

I was there for the termination.
      Can you understand what this means?
            It was the way an entire horse,

the whole animal, spills from the arc
      of a horseshoe to the hole of a nostril,
            the way that the flowing biology must end

in space, must navigate uncertain
      boundaries with ground and air—privacy
            must mean less for the dead—

but I did not look when the ashes
      were blowing, even though I knew
            when they were released, exactly.

Little Break

The Ushuaia tomb upstages
its main display in a glass case:

a nine-foot wing, fallen from a great angel,

quietly jagged at the seam
where the wing met—what?

The back? The shoulder? The other
wing? The shoulder blade, it seems,

for so attached, even a faint
rustling would lift a sorrowing giant,

straighten a spine bent by prayer—Dear,

your shoulder blades do suggest
buds of the folded or forgotten,

but finally, I fear, it's ridiculous
to imagine us in flight!

How much easier to see us here
by the glass and a heavy,
dead wing, too full for flight

—birds and bats have hollow bones,
a void as old as the pterosaur—

how much easier to press the glass,
to gaze down upon the break
as neither act nor scene, but encore:

a pleasing return to an empty stage,
summoned by our own applause—

praise rustled from our battered hands,
which press and release and always seek.

Paean
The Flightless Bird

It could be said she lacks
        one axis—no barbs cross-
stitch her splintered feathers,
        no keel crosscuts her
still-trussed sternum—she
        has little room for flight—

so this is what happens
        when the barbs are gone! Let
other birds sever their
        shadows from high down on
whatever's been slung
        between rooftops to dry—

She riddles the dark down
        her body. Her feathers
sift light from air, layer
        warmth where her wings would be.
She brings upon herself
        six thousand shadows and

forty shades, easily.
        Her eggshells reflect saf-
fron. Let the other birds
        trail their rings of air; the
rhea lifts calm from wind.
        Then shifts the calm closer in.

Torch Song for the World's Second-Oldest Still-Running Wooden Rollercoaster

It looks suspicious: story on story of splintering cross-stitch
buffeted up over tuft and trash. And it sounds even worse—

When the trains take their turns, each nailed X unhitches
a blizzard of clicks, rehearsal of flange—perverse

in its spittle, curmudgeon of thunder—trundle down the boards (four
by sixes) and eventually under the screams veering

past our sun-baked line. We empty pockets, ditch hats, dump plush for this:
the gift that old wood gives to math: here, nearing

free-fall; here, caught and slingshot again, by this scaffold to calculus,
between max and min—naked of plaster, rid of lath, just rib racket and brake—

so the cars with their charges take the slope: the slow clicking advance
coasting the rise, unrolling the hover, plunging between arcade and lake.

Tanda with Jeanette MacDonald Close-up

Her face, since colorized, still burns my eyes:
                eye-green and hair-red gently bled
to the same gray by black and white, and blurred

on screen by Vaseline on the camera
                lens. Or so runs this urban myth of fuzz
and luminosity. Her teeth gleam screen-worthy

white, abut the abyss of her open
                mouth, which houses a swallowing
black. Nelson Eddy will soon arrive

beneath her window to intercept
                her high note, to call her, wrongly,
Blue-eyes. I wait and wait impatiently

for the one who will come for me
                as Nelson will appear, magnificently,
and expose L.A. living rooms in their matinee

to his crashing *Au revoir, Rose Marie!*
                But first, shining from the window
and screen, there flashes the glass—

our signal scudding pixels—
        light flooding Jeanette's lips,
so first out and under I'll go,

—••◦❯❮◦••—

since soon I'll be ten again and doing again

what I really should not, with a boy
        (he was twelve, I'll call him Scott)
and a magnifying glass, under a bush in the backyard,

and soon we'll be caught, and caught very hard, but not before
        we learn how to make night simply,
scrambling and splaying under some shrubbery,

and not before we find that, even beneath
        that bubble of lens, the leaves bleed
their green to shade, and the plump raspberries

lose their red, and not before we turn the lens
        to the diminishing colors
of so many withins: pockets and tank-tops

and dropping-down seams. Mostly not before:
        I find how to lie back in that scratchy, pithed night
and Scott's lens finds one shaft of light

from down the shifting tree and plays its vanishing
        radius rainbow, and mostly not before
the light finds me.

Au revoir, Rose Marie! and then the parting and the flood
        —all the light and still no colors—just the mud
beneath the nails and just the not-night ground

and baths and living-room scales—

So now, obscenely, when I see
        the heady close-up of any Rose Marie,
she has Scott in her teeth,

his towel her fringed handkerchief,
        his clear glass lens swelling the note
that saw his safe passage from the city

center to the fringe of Los Angeles:
        the beach. The ocean splashes sand on sand,
foams green at his feet, stung red

by the wind. Seaweed sprawls in the draw.
        He slaps his board down on its shadow.
He balances black, breaches in.

Mussels

Blue inside
obsidian, blue of compression,
blue of the fleck

and of flash-
cooled glass. We anchor,
volcanic and fast.

We embrace
and make changeful our
beach. We bury.

Between, we
breach—our numbers our
reach—but do

not be fooled
by the forfeit of blue,
that sad shadow mim-

icry shift-
ing on waves, or within.
Not slate nor

azure, we
are devotion to tidal
recession,

we turn to the
backing away of the ocean
as cicadas

turn to their
seventeenth year, as delphinia
gravely follow

the sun, not
unlike some seraphim long
after faltering.

Churchill Blues

Enter Caliban with a burden of wood
Enter Caliban with a burden of wood
       Enter a man with a decision to be made

To save the city and lose the enemy plan?
To lose the city and save the hard-won plan?
       Exit one, the monster or the man

To save the city is to lose the war
To lose the city is to save the war
       Enter one, who exited before

The wounded are dying between the lines
The wounded are dying between the lines
       When I waked, I cried to dream again

All night, all night, the city or the war? Right
is right. No man's an island—Live with it—
       The island's full of sounds that hurt not

Hurt not, hurt not, death-
less peace, hurt not, hurt not, less death
       Prayer or profanity, the same breath—

Set me free, my decision is sent
Set me free, my decision is sent
       Take hands, the curtain's falling. Exuent.

Torch Song for Strangelove with Phrase by Schuyler

Because one B-52 is never enough,
the bomber must drop an H-bomb;
but a stray, knavish nuke is also not enough,
so the pilot (tense, Texan) must muster his moxie, stuff
the maudlin bomb between his legs, and sit
his steel steer pretty as the plane at last shits
both out to the backlit sky and beyond—to the late cut
(big board, Pentagon), where the peacekeepers sniff
out each others' feature-length lousy
diplomacy, and the ist-er-Deutsch? freak flaps his frowzy
yawp and battles his what's-wrong-with-it? limb,
wheeling circles around our worry, cozy and dim,
nudging us to mosey in, sing along,
Vaudeville, vaudeville, world gone wrong.

Good-bye Love Song with Phone and Urn

Portable phones strike me as criminal.　　Take
my great-aunt:　　dying.　　On the phone.
She insists on fretting. She paces. She must make
all her own arrangements, then make them known
to me.　Her mind changes incessantly:　No wake,
three wakes.　Scattered ashes, urn;　headstone,
unmarked grave;　plain slab.　For her sake,
I answer.　　I listen, offer inscriptions.　My own
taste runs to modest;　she prefers epic.
We argue translations, Homer or Virgil.
We talk ourselves into the ground.
She's not called yet today.　She's sick,
I know, perhaps slept in.　I will
call her.　I must read her the passage I have found.

Good-bye Love Song for My Grandmother's Walks

Months since her stroke, and just tonight
my father told me how his mother, still

in her eighth month, still in Riga, fell
and landed on the child she felt

inside her falling still. And how, years
later, in their East Hollywood stairwell,

he would stand and marvel that he'd caught
the whole of his mother before he was born,

but, no matter what, could not will
himself to catch whatever was brought

down upon his own half-brother; he could only warn
his sister away, then follow her, still

raging at his mother's part
in the beating of that house. This was the way

he knew, tonight, how he should stand
by her hospital bed: apart,

tracing the lines of her dead right hand,
lacing her fingers to ease their splay.

Song for a Vanished Grandfather's Possible Houses

for Elmars Paegle

Since I woke, four places
I've never been
have emerged from
the edges of morning.

In the fireplace, on an ashen
hill, a glowing Sarcomonte—
the view of the tombs
from the Alhambra, at dusk—

from the woodpile,
a thin curl of green smoke
urging, *Give him*
an alm, woman,
since there is nothing in this life
like being blind in Granada—

But there is no blind child,
only a charmed swamp thickening
in the frozen grass, steaming to
an Alabama coast—

My sister may have walked
here, her ninth month of pregnancy,
her eighteenth year, growing
along the shore—

But there is no ocean,
only the bathtub claws staggering
under the curving blue belly
of a dreaming giant,
receding into the fever
of the world,

and no scraping moraine,
only a distant sound like
your voice among the ice,
finally, no ice flowers either,
just a wind in the hallway,
and a widening expanse—

the Great Rift Valley
blowing away,
uncovering its bones.

La Primera Nieve

for my mother

Ancient lake bottoms, exposed in half-light.
The dash scratches static, a flash of *no snow*
until nightfall, then news spotty as this light,
fog-caught, vague, something about a satellite,
incredible frictions—and then you find love
on the a.m. West Desert, twilight,
but we're back in B.A., two elevator flights
up, *adentro*, a Victrola sobs a tango,
cóctel y amor, it is the first tango
you sang to us at night, *Y todo a Media Luz,*
que es un brujo el amor, on the air-
waves, long waves, racing in atmosphere,

each basin and range. The music is out there,
though unheard. Here song is different with air,
so the air itself must change—*a Media Luz*
los besos, a Media Luz los dos—the air
is a caress, *a piropo is a stare;*
ignore it, still it has its way with you. So
let them proposition. The boys with flair
always addressed you: *I'll trade your daughter*
for my father. I pledge he's adept in love,
and in decent shape. A gigolo makes love
with his eyes, his words, shivering the dim air
that parts us until it *is* itself a man, go-
ing away, then circling around, advancing a tango

of transparency, a spiral stare, dancing imagined tango
in *crepúsculo interior*, and all this through the *air*—
over seven lanes of traffic—tango
spilling from each corner, from each car—
including this one, now, what seems light-
years away from B.A. And here tango
flickers through the desert, on the dash, in tango
hay de todo, that city, these sands, this snow-
less February first, high and dry, and the snow
that's been promised, even the abrupt dead air
seems a mere rest, part of a song half in love
with easeful death—*La Cumparsita, most beloved*

of all tangos, makes of death a kind of love,
a masked parade of miseria, a tango,
a song—how else to survive in Buenos Aires?
Sudden buzzing, dead air, crackling, *winter snow*
warning for the entire state, freeze—you shove
the dial off, put your sunglasses in the glove
box, blink furiously in what's left of the light:
rearview mirrors patch ovals of western light
in the black east, where they pool, lake-caught light
burning water between salts. *What little love*
I first had for this place—Some part of the love
that left you sick for home. *Recordando*
el pasado que lo hace sufrir. Memory, like snow,

is a scattering of light, *dolor* made crystal. Snow
itself the afterglow of a thing above
it, a thing risen, stilled a minute, then grow-
ing as it disperses, falls; the family scattered through
Spain, Argentina, the States, this desert, its quiet after the tango
is over. And home always a hemisphere away, though
in the same mountain range, the same rain-shadow
as your childhood summers sped from Buenos Aires
to join your father (*for a while, to disappear*)
in Miraflores, where we passed each new year
in air not unlike this, near Salt Lake, but there, no snow
ever—here, this winter is merely late,

a full month past the first of the year, half-light
of spring well on its way, bidden in the air,
changed and changing between flakes—*el amor
es un brujo*—you were nineteen on this shore, tango-
mad but bewitched by a blizzard, your first snow.

tango liso

My God, a verse is not a crown . . . it cannot vault, or dance, or play
—*George Herbert,* The Temple

1. Spain
(Barcelona, 1888)

World Fair. Parakeets and mummers sipping fire.
A few gilded million ramble the streets,
weaving through statuary: L'Arc repeats
some *Triomf*; Columbus points across the water;

seraphim flood a square. Life-sized statues stir
to watch a human tower climb itself: fifteen flights
of flesh. Here, the body stops. Then reverses its
spell in the air; the climbers turn younger

each tier—how they grow down! A whole parade
follows, each harlequin climbing on an older child
until time runs backwards below, dawn made

to set over Aragon's morose, feudal wild.
An adulteress erupts from oil, tears rising, is unbound.
A coronation wanders off; its queen has been uncrowned.

2. Argentina
(Catamarca Province, Sierra Ancasti, 2003)

Oro. A nation you wandered, jade queen
in your pocket. *Eighteen thousand feet above*
the Atlantic, and there was the vein—every lucid noon
you've ever seen, shot through bedrock in a cave—

but you had not phoned about the gold.
A hemisphere away, you talked chess and fossils: a giant
wave of backbone, tucked into summit, each strange joint
like Ancasti in its range, or a fold

in your bandoneón, which this week fell silent
and has been lost, along with the bones you found
years ago, climbing on a moving mountain,

stumbling on placers of gold and beyond the earth's end,
sky-cast, the earth's own shadow—Tío, Tío, now that you're gone,
who will play chess with the dead? I can pretend—

3. United States
(Manhattan, the Equitable Building, 1914)

Playing chess with the dead across an island's
grid, the architects replace old skyscrapers. They fell
the first. Capture its square. Erect a forty-storied spell
in tiers of steel—the highest yet—in tropospheric end-

game rapture. Thirtieth floor: bound cranes bend
to their landings, tying ton to ton, a mile
tricked back into its skeleton. Men rivet miracle
from foot-wide I-beams, a killing wind

blasting up from the Hudson. Lunch is a tight-
rope with no net, skyline spiking like a crown.
Each worker from his shadow is dizzily split

across a vertical board—rank and file, in place of wall.
Ten men eat on a wire. Look down:
ten more tiers of men climbing nothing at all.

4. Spain
(San Sadurní, Human Towers, 2002)

The ten-year-old Rubio is climbing nothing
on this street. Not for family, fanfare,
his friend's hashish, or, equally dubious, village honor.
And Disneyland, though promised, is all wrong.

The troupe from his village will have to get along
without him. They can pull another
climber from somewhere, make a smaller
tower, whatever. But he is passing

out on his side, nose tucked to knees, rinsed
in chills, sinking in old fear of the human
tower collapsing, fifty bodies hitting the square,

plunging with him through brilliance condensed
and streaking cliffs of color, somewhere close to the sun,
lying on the ground, falling from there—

5. Argentina

(Buenos Aires, Eva Perón, 1945)

Don't lie about abandoned ground. I come from there.
This veranda's better. In its vista, stricken with rain,
we can see our valenciennes copied by thunder-
heads over the city. Buenos Aires! Clear

evenings, I watch lovers linger in the park,
embracing each other but fingering the dark—
some quicken at curfew without going in.
Sometimes I drive from this city,

through the pampas or the south.
I memorize the never-never of this terrain: cerulean
rise, blizzarding ravine. Laws, dictated, must be obeyed.

I walk among my people, counting off mouths
beneath the gallows tree. They won't come for me.
I'm no sham. I am not afraid.

6. United States
(Lady Day's Hollywood Earthquakes, 1945)

Unafraid   no sham in white satin   that day you almost died
smoking away your toothache beneath the palm tree
that came thrashing down just after Mac pushed you aside
and you   songbird   flew as the quake crashed the party

in great rolling waves   chandeliers liquefied   split slope
the pool water bubbling over like the champagne
you sipped through your first earthquake   with Bob Hope
and you hated champagne   though you still with each tune

sip air   then give it back in sighs and murmurs now stored
whispering to Frank and everyone alongside your keyboard
to the very earth breaking blue beneath your voice   Sing

again your flight the day you didn't die   *almost* a world of word
to slip through   not your time yet Lady   though we've heard
ever since   in your breath   veiled in blues   another land opening

7. Spain

(Aragon, Katharine Betrothed, 1488)

Infanta in her homeland, far from death and the veils
she'll wear for the journey between Spain and the country
to which she's been betrothed, just barely, in near-nudity—
three years old and diapered in a title: Princess of Wales.

Ringing Princess and dais, a full tournament regales
the Ambassadors, who, to save their dynasty,
spare no bombast. They leave heaping heraldry
on her red-gold head, in the midst of pageantry, bells

floating Spanish galleons across the sea, where she,
fast fourteen behind a veil, meets the seventh Henry
and becomes the first of six queens taken by his son;

five discarded, two beheaded. Now she's greeting everyone,
and England loves her, veil and all, with ball and banquet.
Henry bends to raise her veil and face a silhouette—

8. Argentina
(La Boca, 1944)

When he goes down, she kicks up; her flitting silhouette
spikes heel-to-toe for him to climb, up the terra firma
of her slit-splitting thigh, a slippery vision in set
steps, backward ochos of evasion, then rush and murmur

of advance. Each blink a bet; each salida snaps a threat; the fugitive
sweet nothings in this dance, vaguely avian but made for men,
all cocky preening in sure, wide stance. Still for her all get, little give,
some sidling bandoneóns, a shift of shins, then stripped dipping, deadpan.

They trade tokens of affection: stiff upper lip for jaw-locked mask.
Hand grasps hand; his hand clasps her back; her hand transects
his fancy slants—all the silver gestures relinquished and taken, ask
of the body this answer, this dance, this steady, barely checked hex

unsashed, this hush, this rushing, this fight and flight floored,
this lusty nunc stans, ravished accord.

9. United States
(Denali, "First Female Ascent," 1947)

Subzero gust. Summit. She's famished. But ecstasy, accord-
ing to Hollywood, sells, so the film crew's caught it—
what a climax!—Barbara Washburn, in black and white:
a broad on top of the world. She waves. Gives the word,

and Brad lowers her over the peak, cord-
strung to his public summit, eclipsed for a blessed minute
from the cameras above. Below: cirrus. Ice lacing air. This shot
is all for her, and it's virga to boot—O, to piss like a bird!

Privacy widening, she lingers between God
and the tundra floor, finding the border between nadir
and zenith, a range's peaks and valleys in far air immersed,

a feverish kite, a pale jet stream, a shivering. Odd,
hiding inside the world's wide panorama, to be the first
woman to epistle this sky, *I am here.*

10. Spain
(Katharine of Aragon, Divorced, 1536)

I am the first. I am here. *Thou art alone.* O Griffith,
I'm sick to death. My legs bow to the earth.
Go thy ways, Kate. Nothing but death
shall divorce my dignities. *The queen of earth-*

ly queens. His promises were, as he was then,
mighty. We are a queen—*Good lady, make yourself mirth*—
or long have dreamed so, we are the daughter of a king, certain.
Would I had never trod this English earth.

I can no more. Good Griffith, cause the musicians to play me
that sad note. *Be sad as we would make ye. Men's evil manners
live in brass*—The times and titles are altered strangely
with me—*their virtues we write in water.*

Be well contented to make your house our tower.
My drops of tears I'll turn to sparks of fire.

11. Argentina
(Buenos Aires, Eva Proposes, 1945)

Your drops of tears I'll turn to sparks of fire—
dry your eyes. What king begs for mercy
from his generals? A messy
coup this was, indeed. Have a gin. I tire

of quiet tidying. All people require
is some small controversy,
some token. Do me this courtesy.
In fencing, you aim for the heart. Desire

what your people desire—shirtless in
chivalry—they pull weeds, count beads, sin
the better to see their neighbor's sin. Demand

a rematch. Have another. Stand.
Your practice is sufficient—better on your knee.
Fall's upon us, but spring is coming. Lie to me.

12. United States
(Manhattan, the Equitable Re-Christened, 1915)

O fall upon us, Holy Spirit,
in this spilling of wine.
Break it open, George. Let
us pray. Lord, keep near

to you this building. Crown
its old skyline inside it, so we can christen
it again: the Highest. Hurray
for Al and his crew. Amen.

It was tough to get a blessing today.
The bit about two buildings was nice.
How alone, this skyscraper, otherwise—
After all, what surrounds us up here?

Distance flying from itself. Best
to let a thing have its ghost.

13. Spain
(Barcelona, Sagrada Familia, 1996, 1936, 1926)

The passion façade gives up its ghost
again, *Guernica* in stone. Civil war is babble
on the other side of us, the whole host
sundered, the family gone to scaffold.

The towers throw broken gold, *hosanna* and *excelsis*
over the poor, mosaics soar, rosaries, words
strung up for God. Between wars, Antoni pieces
out magi, salamanders, a nativity warm with birds.

June. He's counting towers still unbuilt: thirteen.
Apostles, Mary, Christ. In the pauper's hospital,
St. Barnabus is visiting. Antoni begins to refuse

again—he won't give up his bed—but between
thought and voice, he already has; his cathedral
vivid with all it's still missing, *sanctus sanctus sanctus*

14. Argentina
(Buenos Aires, Depression, 2003)

The mall is vivid with what it's missing; everything
has stopped. Pinballs winter apart from their orbits
in the guttered dust of machines; the Ferris wheel sits,
its somnolence an elaborate, chance smoke ring

looming above the dead food court. Stranger things
have happened: outside, the middle class squats
to trade trash. A doctor shoos sewage down streets.
A girl begs with gusto, tune of a tango. She can sing.

This sets her apart from the others—mutilated, ill—
according to her padre. She's missing an arm, one ear.
All day, she's waited without luck, and only three smokes.

Now her profile—half-lit by the doctor's match—is "regal."
Why not? The city has a miracle coming, and she expects her share.
Her address is gone, and smoke is a signal—Whatever it takes.

15. United States
(Construction Site, Lower Manhattan, 2003)

The address is gone. The world is near,
or a nation away, wandering past the queen
across the harbor, who stays with the dead—
In ten years, five towers will climb over void,

will belie their ground. From here, we fall into war,
wild with terror, fighting what we can't see, trading
dead for dead—*homeland, homeland*—that veil—
as if each strange ghost gives up a fleeting silhouette

instead of air over this ground—adding to a sum replete.
What is *here*? Not the first, nor men's last evil,
written in brass—*their virtues we write in water*—

which falls upon and from us. Spring is coming.
When what stays is as vivid as what is missing: heat
or prayer, a force moving silence *about to sing.*

choir

Whoever is outside his fatherland is a pilgrim, whereas in a narrow sense one of us is not called a pilgrim unless he is journeying toward the sanctuary of St. James of Compostela or is returning therefrom.

—*Dante,* Vita Nuova

St. Iago de Campus Stellae
Timeline

The cathedral of Santiago de Compostela, or St. James of the Field of Stars, houses the world's largest censer, three feet in radius. The censer's size allows for the purification of the cathedral from its pilgrims, who visit, unwashed and road weary, in large numbers.

—*Brochure*

800   Star shower, cave dream.
          A hermit, a vision,
               a found apostle's tomb; little hidden church
     in the mountain. Architecture among
             dolomite. Atmosphere alight.

1200   Excavation of found-
          ation. A vision, a na-
             tion, clerical succession; little hidden moun-
       tain moved. Architecture among
            dolomite. The construction site.

1600   Excavation of found
          nation. A shore, an a-
             merica, stolen silver, gold; precious hidden met-
       als removed. Ornament among archi-
            tecture. The pilgrimage site.

1999   Watershed of pilgrimage
            routes. Cockleshells mark
                the Pyrenees, converge; living rivers down mountains
         move. Pilgrimage among pilgrims.
                Silver censer alights,

1999.9   falls with the moment-
            um of a wrecking ball, reflect-
                ion of a Foucault pendulum gone mad; count-
        erweight greater than gravity or rotation. Scale
                among scales. The rite

1999.99 of purification, from moment, from
            road-sleep sweat, by the big-
                gest censer in the world, smashing—diminishing
        interval moves into convergence—among—
                smoke moves pilgrims into atm-

1999.99o9   sphere   Alight.

Aizpute Dome

for Alfred Dinne, February 3, 1925–December 9, 2003

2000.
Eleven years since the Wall fell; and the millennium dispelled
        itself like church bells rung in the small town where
you were born. Standing under the Aizpute Dome before we called
        you in the States from your homeland, Grandfather,
how we practiced all our questions; how we again mulled
        what we'd always wondered: When you fled Latvia, were
        you fifteen? Was it June? Did you see your family killed
from the field where you hid—the field where we just gathered asters?

Were you alone? What happened, those four years, between
        leaving Latvia and arriving in the one story we all know well:
How, in a Displaced Persons camp, at the age of nineteen,
        you first met Grandmother and her two small
children, her husband lost, starving; their ill boy (our father) refusing
        all food in his fever, reduced to simple whimpering for apples, *abols*,
no fresh food to be had until, in the half-light of a half-moon,
        that midnight in June, Grandmother was visited, as she loved to tell,

by *a hunched old man*, how then you straightened and were young
        and humming, how you shrugged from your back bags of apples stolen
from some distant guarded field, apples certain, apples real, how his lungs
        cleared, and how suddenly he healed, and how she knew then,

that survival could be simple, that it was a thing stolen, sudden, and slung
       from a stranger's shoulders—*if survival is temptation, hunger is the greater sin*—
and that turning from hunger was as close to heaven as she wanted to come
       in this life, in which all you would ever say about Aizpute when asked, was, *Heaven.*

When we finally called you from your town—here is the photo of me
       on the phone, in the booth, across from the field—how you let it ring
and ring, and by the time you at last picked up, cantankerous, gruffly
       humming along to your TV, blaring another choir, so their singing
eclipsed our intended questions, the nearer Aizpute bells, all we nearly
       asked before you cut us off with your own requests: *Bring*
yourselves back. Forget the asters. What's that racket in the background? Be
       quiet, listen, you'll hear June. Aizpute is where midsummer comes from: hidden in its green.

Köln

for Antonia Dinne

1.

1985. We three sisters believe this city in West Germany comes as close
        as we can ever be
    to the city that seems never to have lived
        outside those sisters' memories

in Germany our grandmother is known as *Antonia*   the eldest of her three
She has brought her son's daughters from Los Angeles here if only to see
    what's left of Europe   her white gloves float toward us when we

2.

race across the square to where the youngest sister Milda beckons
bare-handed   her smile
    opera-diva wide   humming her still-well-known tremolo   inside
    outside   across   the cathedral and her adopted Germany
    how we adore her air baths   her canaries   her LPs   her
    singing irrepressible   her operas   her adopted blues
    even the old folksongs   most of all we   half-ashamed
        entirely adore her
    ease undeniable even in her pauses mid Autobahn   arrested by some
    radio
    recitative here   her wave   an electric aria   flash of palm there
    hailing   across the

space of cathedral square   across   we perceive
the   ocean to New York
            where the middle sister Lidija estranged herself from her own
            family   we see her

trace   glinting as we run   breaking into the

lace between the birds' bodies as they scatter to sky   in the
windows rising between their
            wingtips   reflected as in her own window   her hand
its wave

                        very like   between birds   a good-bye   something
like love

3.

for Riga
Riga shattered   for Milda in a million frenzied chords

Riga scattered from the camps   for Lidija hiding her husband beneath blankets
            and boards

Riga must no longer matter for Antonia in the shadow of erratic masts and
            her own deft steps waltzing down the casements west on the ship
            that carried across an ocean her steps   steps started
            marching two babies from Riga and finally left

Europe with her husband Elmars's last letter addressed from the military
        hospital *please send food*   *the Latvian Resistance is starving*
        after six years of Displaced Person's camps
Hollywood's palm trees seem sufficient   semblances of heaven

4.

Now the organist is pounding out an aria of Bach's
        and the sky amasses clouds that suggest a coming storm
evaporated perhaps from the Baltic Sea   amber in waves
                in rain
      risen in skies   irreverent of boundaries

5.

Today Milda says the bones of the Wise Men
        are entombed here behind the cathedral's battered
           façade—below   the street men
    layer their chalks jade-eyed Christs make sacred
           the pavement   marking an unwalkable
  space   while above the buttresses remember war

Today I thought I almost touched
        the aura worn by strangers just before
    a first meeting   that bloom   known only after its fade
             into the familiar
    face and later remembered   in another place

        as eminent newness that fled before   affinity—Here the Magi

dwell in eminence   Here their bones embrace
          the escaping newness of each passing age
each   erases   their remains a little bit more

So it is with this city
          its receding streets are so often steeped in strangeness
                              its doors forever flee their rooms' sudden
          grace   and its buttresses   from the Magi's bones   continuously soar

Köln's steeples fly

                    to fling down their shadows—
                                        newness
                         familiarity
                    forgetting
          and each shadow touches each Christ

                         slanting   into the chalk   of always another
          place

Clock and Echo

Confession is the better communion—

no stale wafer flattened on the palate, there stung with acid wine—

       I'll take the tight body of wood
anointing my sins anytime: echo beginning.   My own words

     muffled, made familiar, made sound and sin and part
of the marble that makes cathedral dome
        hold sky—what oiled wood can do to words!

What snow falling can do to morning.   What space in a bed can do *to recline*.

       Some time before this morning
we lay in the aftermath of our overture.
      There was a fire.   The strings inside the piano still

hummed. A box, a harp, some keys by a fire.
     And your restored   grandfather clock, its missing pendulum
swing-dancing the air. Your
      flush like a woman. You loved
that you were more beautiful than I. Well, you too would have

grown old—still, we did establish an
        intimacy. You knew what there is
                to know of my body, where time gathers, where it lies.

You were remarkably present
        in the important moments of the body.
                And you thought the priests could still be shocked.

So we return to St. John. So back to the Divine. So I miss that a building

can hold so much sky—all that rock rising
                    just to bring some space inside—and here is

what I know of this morning: snow is falling in sheaths and columns. Hidden
        priests are always becoming
beautiful. The sun is distant and the temperature is falling. Soon the snow
will fall in crystals and pile on the leaves piled on the lawn, and soon some
priest will welcome our desire, and his shock will always be sublime. Soon
        the days will shift down the hours, obscuring the evening
            and lighting the dawn, and
soon there will be no need to write of priests or leaf piles, since very soon
        now I will write, *now that you are gone—*

Rome has set

precedents few follow.
Consider its insist-
ence on size—even its hist-
ory is big. Although
broken—collective shadow
of cats in the coliseum, list
of the names that persist,
sainted a few millennia ago.
Consider the great
St. Peter's, for instance.
Then consider the ways
the feral cats mate,
multiplying a silence
that breeds and stays.

Montserrat Tour

In the legend, this is the cave
filled with green light, insisted
upon by the Mother of God—
she loved again and again to deceive

the shepherds who tried to move
her down-mountain—she'd
stay with them but fade
with each step and so never arrive

on the plains. For intercessions,
saints are more steady. During
vespers, though, Mary's still best

—when the *salve montserinna* begins,
my cousin says he can see her green
flash, all the way from Key West.

Another Reason the Tree on Seventh South and Third East Weeps

In spring the Virgin Mary appeared in Salt Lake City, on a stormy night in the barrio near downtown. . . . Centered in the circle of the tree's old wound was the silhouette of the Virgin of Guadalupe, slick with rain. . . . It became apparent that what poured from her image were her tears, which came both from her eyes and from the region of her heart.

—*Mark Doty,* Firebird

Boomerang, Daphne.
                             Trees are still good

places for receding

         when so many gods are obsessed with coupling,
when anything else is flight.

            When anything else
is tree, sap, trappings,
         water into sugar

behind striped alterations of xylem—
              phloem, xylem, *anything else*
is cambium, any ring only cross section,
        age under scrutiny, not orbit, not the starry arms
of galaxy. *But that laurel tree?*

Has learned the coefficients over centuries.
Can discern her isograds
under spongy ground
cover. *Knows where change*
meets percolating air, because now
she is there—

leaking from sugar to surface,
       down to fingertips, coffee cans, groundwater.

Defying surface tension,
       defying phloem, preparing for metamorphism.

Her spirit has crystallized.
       Her spirit is about to rise

                                     verse: re

turn.

Estuary and Divide
Fiambala: Cueva de la Virgin, Catamarca, Argentina
for Maria del Valle de Acuña, May 13, 1917–January 23, 2007

Not far from that shore
          here spans a cave,
                stunned with silver through its thresholds—
    milagro upon milagro hanging in the absence
        of ailment and two hundred tons of rock,
   stalagmites spangled in miniature
limbs bent and battered in metal, picking up candlelight and miracle—

       miracles that always occur in spite
               of themselves and divide
the self from faith—
       this row of small silver caves, eye
of a needle—
       these dangling feet
           should not need any shining
idols—this column will grow around the curving gray arms—
      when the sea rushes the cave again—
         will grip the dented metal hearts—

At tidewater,

        reeds rise

     from riverbottom to this: self-
        parting at the surface, where insects skid and jump valences:
substance split to ions,
     electric sleights of shadow ripple down the waters, shadow and all
muted by ground fog or mist or troposphere dropped and scattered—

     around these reeds,
            where they wear their shadows,
                      some silver—

hand, lung, two horses—

That they float on salt
in the shadow of a reed *is*
faith and not its caving, not its insistence, but the quiet litter of its
presence,
that they are here where river bottoms out to the sea,
where the waters mix salt with crushed mountains, pounding out the quartz—

this is for everything that parts in moving, reed, tuft, river—

that these small made pieces
made their way here, to this place
in the moon's pull,
dull, among water beetle and mist—

Latvian Boys' Choir

for my father

—So many wrists, such a short life
lodged in that part of the arm, held

stiffly at the side of song; such a brief
respite between breath and *forte*—Wild,

lean notes of aria tunnel the air between
the boys' small bodies: bodies of wrist

and of song, bodies gasped and wished and hinting
the steady risen rapture of the Riga Dome—

conjured and convincing, staggered on the stairs
before the single flashing hand of the metronome—

and eleven years (their lifetime!) after their amethyst
shore glowed from Tallinn to Vilnius and the prayers

of their parents who assembled—two million strong—
and sang—human chain in occupation—their songs.

Notes

Canto de Abril

The phrase "caserón antiguo" and the rhythm of this broken villanelle are influenced by the folkloric song "Zamba de Abril," written by Chango Rodríguez. The phrase "life too dim without illusion" is a loose translation of lyrics from "Sapo Cancionero," by Jorge Hugo Chagra and Nicolas Toledo.

The Plaza de Mayo was the scene of the May 25, 1810, resolution that led to Argentina's independence from Spain and has remained a focal point of political life in Buenos Aires. Since 1977, the plaza has been used by the Mothers of the Plaza de Mayo, who meet weekly to commemorate their children who were "disappeared" by the Argentine military in the Dirty War—the state-sponsored violence against the Argentine citizenry from 1976 to 1983.

The Plaza was also prominent during the eras of Juan Dominguez Perón and Eva Perón. On October 17, 1945, Evita and the labor union led mass demonstrations, culminating in the release of Juan Perón from prison. Since then, the Plaza has served as both a gathering place for Perón's supporters and a target for his critics. The Peróns' complicated legacy still divides many Argentine families, some of which, like my own, include both supporters and victims of the Peróns.

Paeans

These poems are all inspired by animals native to Argentina, many of which are endangered. The exception is the beaver, which was imported from Canada to Tierra del Fuego by the Argentine government in the 1940s. Since then, the beaver have dominated the island.

Churchill Blues

This poem explores Winston Churchill's alleged decision to sacrifice the city of Coventry to the German Luftwaffe Air Force in order to protect a decisive source of intelligence. Although historians still contest whether Churchill knew of the air raid on Coventry in time, the decision remains a crux of wartime statecraft.

La Primera Nieve

The Spanish phrases are taken from the tango "A Media Luz," by Carlos César Lenzi and Edgardo Donatto. The propagation of radio waves through the Earth's atmosphere is altered by changes in the ionization of the atmosphere by solar flares, geomagnetic storms, and other electromagnetic events and by sudden changes in the atmosphere's vertical moisture. Under such conditions, radio broadcasts can reach far beyond their normal range.

Tango Liso
"Tango Liso" translates as "Smooth Tango" and refers to the kind of tango popular in the salons in the '40s and '50s—a controlled tango consisting of primary steps and minimal embellishments.

3. United States (Manhattan, the Equitable Building, 1914)
This Second Renaissance Revival building casts a seven-acre shadow over Lower Manhattan. From the National Register of Historical Places: "Erected in 1914–15 . . . the 40-story steel and masonry Equitable Building served as the home office of the Equitable Life Assurance Society from 1915 to 1924. . . . It stands on the site of Equitable's first home office, which was built in 1870 and destroyed by fire in 1912."

6. United States (Lady Day's Hollywood Earthquakes, 1945)
This poem is based upon events narrated by Billie Holiday and William Duffy in Holiday's memoir, *Lady Sings the Blues.*

9. United States (Denali, "First Female Ascent," 1947)
This poem is based upon events narrated by Barbara Washburn during a slide presentation she gave in Denali Park, Alaska, in 1996.

10. Spain (Katharine of Aragon, Divorced, 1536)
This poem is a cut-up of Shakespeare's *King Henry VIII.*

14. Argentina (Buenos Aires, Depression, 2003)
As a result of alternating military dictatorships and weak democratic governments, high public debt, hyperinflation, abrupt neoliberal economic reform, pegging of the Austral to the dollar, dollar flight, unemployment, and a run on banks, Argentina suffered a severe economic crisis between 1999 and 2003.

Köln
Situated on the border of the territories divided up by the Molotov-Ribbentrop pact concluded between the Nazis and the Soviets, Latvia was assigned to the Soviet sphere of influence and was promptly occupied by Russian troops. When Hitler broke this pact in 1941, Latvia was invaded and occupied by the Nazis until the war's end. More than 200,000 Latvians died during this period, including 70,000 Latvian Jews. Having expelled

the Nazis, the Russians reoccupied Latvia until after Latvian independence and did not withdraw all its troops until 1994.

Latvian Boys' Choir

This poem juxtaposes the sequence of protests against Soviet occupation held by Estonians, Latvians, and Lithuanians between 1988 and 1991. These rallies—collectively called the Singing Revolution for the prominent role of folk songs suppressed under the Soviets—were instrumental in the Baltic States' independence.

Acknowledgments

Grateful acknowledgment is made to the editors of the following magazines, anthologies, and publications in which these poems have appeared, sometimes in slightly different forms:

Academy of American Poets Helen Burns Anthology and *New Orleans Review*: "Estuary and Divide"

AGNI: "Tanda in Four Parts with Jeanette McDonald Close-up"

Barrow Street: "Good-bye Love Song with Siroopwafelen" and "Good-bye Love Song with Oil Painting by Randall Lake"

Bellingham Review: "Inside the Bandoneón" as "Sabado, Domingo"; "Little Break"; and "Latvian Boys' Choir"

Best New Poets 2007 and *Cream City Review*: "Clock and Echo"

Colorado Review: "St. Iago de Campus Stellae: Timeline"

Mid-America Poetry Review: "Churchill Blues" and "Good-bye Love Song with Phone and Urn"

Pacific Review: "Good-bye Love Song with the World's Second-Oldest Still-Running Wooden Rollercoaster"

Ploughshares: "Little Break from Iglesia de Nuestra Señora de Pilar," as "A Little Beer during Fence Repair"

Prairie Schooner: the section *Tango Liso*: "Spain (Barcelona, 1888)," "Sierra Ancasti, 2003," "Manhattan, 1914," "San Sadurní, 2002," "Buenos Aires, 1945," "Hollywood Earthquakes, 1943, 2003," "Aragon, 1488," "La Boca, 1944," "Denali, 1947," "Aragon, 1536," "Buenos Aires, 1945," "Manhattan, 1915," "Sagrada Familia, 1996, 1936, 1926," "Buenos Aires, 2003," and "Building Site, Lower Manhattan, 2003"

Southern Review: "Song for Mussels" and "Song for a Vanishing Grandfather's Possible Houses"

Third Coast: "Paean: The Prejudiced Goat"

Western Humanities Review: "Torch Song for Ophelia" and "La Primera Nieve"

Thanks for encouragement and financial support from the Steffensen Cannon foundation, the University of Utah, and the Utah Arts Council.

      For their good words, kind support, and great and lasting guidance, thanks to Katharine Coles, Peter Covino, Disa Gambera, Donald Revell, Tom Stillinger, Kathryn Stockton, Barry Weller, and especially Jacqueline Osherow and Karen Brennan. I will always be grateful to Mark Doty for his early faith and to Agha Shahid Ali for his wit, rigor, and time. Many thanks to Kristen Buckles, editor extraordinaire, and to Juan Delgado for his encouragement and crucial direction. Thanks to Jessica Lewis Luck for her attentive eye and generous ear and to Corinna Vallianatos and Kevin Moffett for their commiseration and camaraderie. My gratitude is extended to Mary Jo Bang, Michelle Boisseau, Joshua Clover, Mark Doty, Judith Hall, and Natasha Tretheway, for their (uncannily timed and sustaining) selection of some of these poems for prizes, awards, and inclusion in anthologies. Thanks to Bret Johnston and Benjamin Percy for their goodwill and support. Thanks to my friends and readers: Jeff Chapman, Nicole Walker, Stephen Tuttle, Kate Rosenberg, Eric Burger, David Hawkins, Kathryn Cowles, Geoff Babbitt, Stuart Greenhouse, Brenda Sieczkowski, Christine Marshall, Ely Shipley, Derek Henderson, Derek Pollard, Jacqueline Lyons, Mike White, Jason McDonough, Trista Emmer, Rebecca Lindenberg, Kelly Le Fave, Maggie Golston, Heidi Czerwiec Blitch, Catharine Wagner, Judy Jordan, and Jenny Mueller. Thank you, my students, from whom I learn every day.

      Many thanks to my family, especially to my grandmother Churita, who translated the manuscript into Spanish several years ago. Most of all, love and gratitude to my parents Jan and Julia for their brilliant examples; my sisters Rita and Christina for their friendship; my niece Alina for her honesty; my young sons Connor and Quinn for their game willingness to share me with my screen time; and always to Steve, for everything.

About the Author

Julie Sophia Paegle lives in the San Bernardino Mountains with her husband Stephen Lehigh and their sons Connor and Quinn. She teaches at California State University, San Bernardino, where she is Poetry Coordinator for the MFA program. She was born in Salt Lake City, Utah, and spent time growing up in Argentina, where her mother was born; she has also returned to Latvia, her father's birthplace. More recently, she divided her time between Alaska and Utah, where she earned undergraduate degrees in Environmental Earth Science and English. She holds an MFA and a PhD in literature and creative writing from the University of Utah. She taught as a poet in the schools and for the University of Alaska–Fairbanks's Upward Bound program, served as poetry editor for *Quarterly West*, and worked as a dog-handler and a wrangler in Alaska.

Her poetry has appeared in various literary journals and anthologies. Recent projects include a book-length poem, *Twelve Clocks*, which attends to loss (from the death of Astyanax to global cycles of mass extinction) by juxtaposing such measures of time as geochronology and mass spectrometry with the traditional epic topos of poetic immortality, and *How We Die in the North*, a memoir that alternates between verse and prose pages to explore the rich array of local myths, legends, and events of the Murphy Dome region north of Fairbanks, Alaska. Her most recent poems are obsessed with the southern California mountains and deserts—their ecosystems, species, droughts, and fires.

Library of Congress Cataloging-in-Publication Data

Paegle, Julie Sophia, 1971–
   torch song tango choir / Julie Sophia Paegle.
      p.   cm. — (Camino del sol)
   ISBN 978-0-8165-2864-6 (pbk. : acid-free paper)
   I. Title.
   PS3616.A3363T67 2010
   811'.6—dc22
                              2010006136